Dragonflies

Trudi Strain Trueit

Cavendish
Square

New York

Published in 2014 by Cavendish Square Publishing, LLC
303 Park Avenue South, Suite 1247, New York, NY 10010

Library of Congress Cataloging-in-Publication Data

Trueit, Trudi Strain.
Dragonflies / Trudi Strain Trueit.
p. cm. — (Backyard safari)
Includes bibliographical references and index.
Summary: "Identify specific dragonflies. Explore their behavior, life cycle, mating habits, geographical location, anatomy, enemies, and defenses"
—Provided by publisher.
ISBN 978-1-60870-244-2 (hardcover) • ISBN 978-1-62712-028-9 (paperback) • ISBN 978-1-60870-818-5 (ebook)
1. Dragonflies—Juvenile literature. I. Title. II. Series.
QL520.T78 203
595.7'33—dc23
2011016329

Editor: Christine Florie
Art Director: Anahid Hamparian
Series Designer: Alicia Mikles

Expert Reader: John C. Abbott, Curator of Entomology at the Texas Natural Science Center, The University of Texas at Austin

Photo research by Marybeth Kavanagh

Cover photo by Bob Jensen/Alamy
The photographs in this book are used by permission and through the courtesy of: *Alamy*: Jim Corwin, 4; Marvin Dembinsky Photo Associates, 22 (C3); *John C. Abbott/Abbott Nature Photography*: 5, 20, 22 (A2, A3, B1), 23 (A1, A2, A3, B2, B3), 27; *Age Fotostock*: Cordier-Huguet, 7TL; *SuperStock*: age fotostock, 7LR, 14LR, 22 (B2); Cusp, 9; James Urbach, 10; Mark Cassino, 12; Animals Animals, 15, 22 (C1, C2), 23 (B1); F1 Online, 16; All Canada Photos, 22 (A1); imagebroker.net, 28; *Cutcaster*: Miro Kovacevic, 13C (boot); Ivan Montero, 13E (binoculars); Sergey Skryl, 13D (camera); Sergej Razvodovskij, 13F (pencils); *Media Bakery*: BigStockPhoto, 13A (hat), 13B (glasses); *Corbis*: Don Johnston/All Canada Photos, 14TL; *AP Photo*: Center for Biological Diversity, 24; *Getty Images*: Sean Justice/Riser, 26

Printed in the United States of America

Contents

Introduction

Have you ever watched baby spiders hatch from a silky egg sac? Or seen a butterfly sip nectar from a flower? If you have, you know how wonderful it is to discover nature for yourself. Each book in the Backyard Safari series takes you step-by-step on an easy outdoor adventure, then helps you identify the animals you've found. You'll also learn ways to attract, observe, and protect these valuable creatures. As you read, be on the lookout for the Safari Tips and Trek Talk facts sprinkled throughout the book. Ready? The fun starts just steps from your back door!

ONE
Flying Gems

You're sitting on the grass in your backyard when something that looks like a tiny green helicopter zips past. There's no mistaking a dragonfly! With their thin, colorful bodies and long, lacy wings, it's no wonder we have given these enchanting creatures names like Mocha Emerald, Sanddragon, and Flame Skimmer.

Dragonflies are among the oldest insects on Earth. Scientists have found dragonfly fossils dating back more than 250 million years, meaning they were around long before dinosaurs. Originally, humans didn't see eye to eye on dragonflies. Some ancient cultures in Eastern Europe feared them. They gave these large, harmless insects names such as devil's darning needles and snake doctors. Still, other people found dragonflies inspiring. In Japan, warriors wore dragonfly emblems on their

Dragonflies have been around for millions of years. This dragonfly is a female Calico Pennant.

helmets to symbolize strength. Many American Indian groups believed dragonflies gave the gifts of strength, courage, and good luck. Today, a dragonfly brings beauty and grace to any yard it visits.

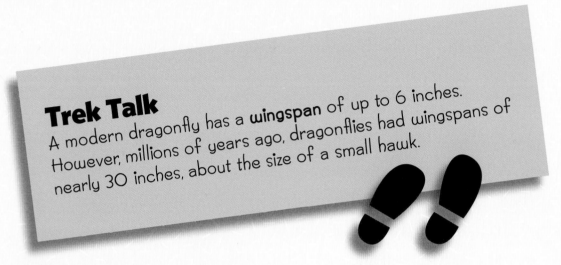

Trek Talk
A modern dragonfly has a **wingspan** of up to 6 inches. However, millions of years ago, dragonflies had wingspans of nearly 30 inches, about the size of a small hawk.

Water Babies

Dragonflies are most often seen near ponds, marshes, streams, or lakes. This is because dragonflies spend more than 90 percent of their lives in the water. A dragonfly's life is made up of three stages: egg, **larva**, and adult. Have you ever seen a dragonfly dipping the tip of its abdomen into a pond? It was likely a female releasing her eggs. After mating, a female dragonfly lays her eggs in the water, in the stems of plants near water, or in muddy soil. Eggs usually take from one to eight weeks to hatch, depending on the type of dragonfly. Some eggs laid in autumn will not hatch until spring.

An adult female Emperor dragonfly releases her eggs into water.

Safari Tip

When you spot a dragonfly, it's okay to go in for a closer look. Their needlelike bodies may seem threatening, but they aren't. Dragonflies don't have stingers and don't usually bite (though they may pinch a bit if held).

A newborn dragonfly is called a larva, nymph, or naiad. It looks like a teeny bug. A larva may spend months or years in the water. It has a clawed, hinged lower lip it uses to catch insects, worms, tadpoles, and even small fish to eat. To grow, it must **molt**, or shed, its **exoskeleton**. A larva will molt between eight and seventeen times.

Dragonfly larvae live in the water for several months before moving to dry land.

7

With each molt, the head, body, legs, and wings slowly develop (larvae cannot fly). Before its final molt, or **metamorphosis**, the larva crawls out of the water. It begins to change from a water insect with gills to one that is able to breathe air. Splitting its last exoskeleton, the dragonfly steps out of its skin. It waits for its wings to inflate and dry, and for its body to harden. Fully grown, it is now ready to take its first flight as an adult. Most adult dragonflies live less than two months, though some Darners and Skimmers may live for nearly a year.

Fabulous Fliers

Dragonflies belong to an order of insects called *Odonata*, meaning "toothed ones." The term refers to a dragonfly's strong **mandibles**, or jaws. Adult dragonflies use their powerful jaws to catch prey in midair. A dragonfly may dart through a swarm of insects with its mouth wide open or form a basket with its long legs to scoop **prey** out of the air. Dragonflies eat whatever they can capture, including mosquitoes, flies, moths, gnats, and other dragonflies. Their excellent eyesight helps in catching a meal. A dragonfly has a pair of eyes so enormous they practically cover its entire head. Each eye may have as many as 28,000 tiny lenses. These large, compound eyes allow the insect to see in almost any direction, including behind it.

Dragonflies have eyes so large they cover most of its head.

Trek Talk
The Mocha Emerald and Prince Baskettail belong to the Emeralds, a family of dragonflies named for their striking green eyes.

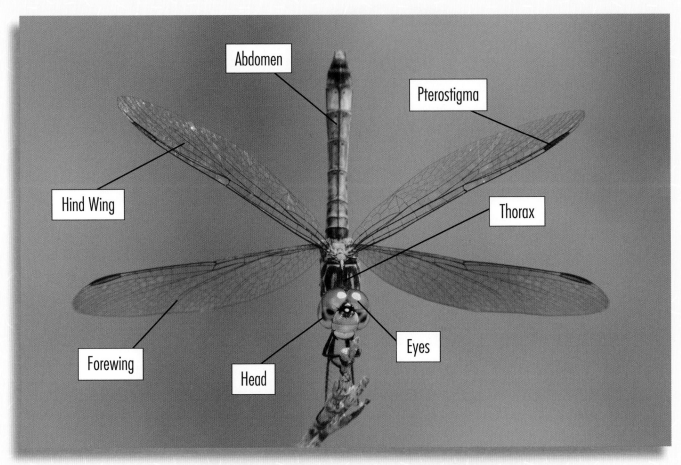

Abdomen

Pterostigma

Hind Wing

Thorax

Forewing

Eyes

Head

Dragonflies are built to fly with long, thin abdomens and four wings.

Dragonflies are among the insect world's best fliers. A dragonfly has four long, see-through wings attached to its thorax. Unlike other insects, it can flap its forewings and hind wings separately. This allows it to fly forward or backward at amazing speeds. Some dragonflies can reach speeds of up to 30 miles per hour. A dragonfly can also quickly change direction or pause and hover in the air for up to a minute (it beats its wings thirty times per second)! Dragonflies are such expert fliers that aerospace engineers are constantly studying them in an effort to improve the wings of man-made aircraft.

Now that you've learned about dragonflies, let's head outside to try to find these flying gems in action.

Dragonfly Destiny

What do some North American dragonflies have in common with some birds and butterflies? They **migrate!** Each fall, many types of Darner and Skimmer dragonflies set out on a long-distance journey. Flying up to 85 miles a day, they travel from Canada and the northern United States to Mexico and the Caribbean. Through their experiments, scientists have discovered that migratory dragonflies stop to rest and don't fly on windy days, just like birds. Experts are still trying to learn, however, just why dragonflies migrate. Does it have something to do with the weather? Habitats? Food sources? Diseases? For now, it's a mystery.

TWO
You Are the Explorer

Although dragonflies can be seen year-round in warm areas, most North American dragonflies take to the sky from May to October. Like butterflies, many dragonflies **bask**, or warm their muscles for flight. So choose a day for your safari when the temperature is above 65 degrees Fahrenheit, the sun is out, and the winds are calm (dragonflies don't like to fly on windy days).

Trek Talk

Scientists aren't certain where the name "dragonfly" came from, but one story suggests it may have originated from an ancient Roman folktale about the devil changing a horse into a flying insect. Today, depending on where you live, you may refer to a dragonfly as a darning needle, devil's needle, snake doctor, spindle, or mosquito hawk.

A Meadowhawk dragonfly soaks up the sun.

What Do I Wear?

* A hat with a brim
* A long-sleeved shirt
* Jeans or long pants
* Waterproof shoes or boots (if you are going near water)
* Sunglasses
* Sunscreen

What Do I Take?

* A pair of close-focusing binoculars (4 to 6 feet)
* Magnifying glass
* Digital camera
* Notebook
* Colored pens or pencils
* Water

Safari Tip
Damselflies (above) are relatives of dragonflies, and one is often mistaken for the other. Here's one way to tell the difference. A dragonfly's forewings are narrower at the base than its hind wings, while the forewings and hind wings of a damselfly are all the same shape.

Where Do I Go?

Dragonflies will be attracted to these things in your backyard:

* Birdbaths
* Fountains
* Large puddles
* Small ponds and streams
* Flowers and vegetables
* Trees, plants, and long grasses
* Logs, sticks, and stumps
* Flat rocks

Look for dragonflies perching on long stems or sticks.

If your backyard doesn't offer these features, here are some other good safari locations:

* ❋ Public lake shores
* ❋ Public parks
* ❋ Open fields
* ❋ Marshes and wetlands

Always have an adult with you if you are going beyond your backyard. Also, whenever you are near water, stay at least 5 feet from the water's edge.

Trek Talk
Dragonflies range in size from the Elfin Skimmer, which is just shy of an inch long, to the Giant Darner, which is 4.3 inches long.

Delightful Darners
Darners are North America's largest, fastest, and most colorful dragonflies. They get their name from their similarity to darning, or large sewing, needles. Darners have bright blue and green body stripes and clear wings. Some Darners change colors with the weather. On hot days, their abdominal stripes turn blue to reflect heat away and keep the insect from overheating. On cool days, the stripes turn dark purple to more quickly absorb the sun's rays. Darners can be found perching on grasses in fields or flying near water.

What Do I Do?

✲ Choose a sunny spot to sit next to flowers, trees, or a water source. Use your binoculars to scan the area for dragonflies. Take a closer look at trees, flowers, and plants with your magnifying glass. Be sure to search the stems of plants, too. This is where many types of dragonflies like to hang out. On a warm day, watch for dragonflies obelisking. Tipping forward, a dragonfly will raise the tip of its abdomen toward the sky in what looks like a handstand (some dragonflies point their abdomens downward). The obelisk posture reduces the amount of sunlight that directly hits the body, helping to keep the insect cooler.

When searching for dragonflies find a good spot that includes things that they like, such as tall grasses. Use your binoculars to scan the area for them.

✳ Snap a photo or make a sketch of the insects you find. If you can, draw or take a photo of the entire insect, from head to tip. This will help you to identify it later.

✳ Make an entry in your notebook. Describe the dragonfly in as much detail as possible. What color is its thorax? How about its long abdomen? Do you see any stripes, rings, or other **field markings** on its body? What color are the insect's wings? Almost all dragonflies have small rectangular markings, called **pterostigmata** (TERR-uh-stig-MAWT-uh), near the tip of each wing. But many dragonflies, like those of the Skimmer family, have additional markings, such as spots, thick bands, and patches. Note the color of the dragonfly's face and eyes, too. Also, write down where you saw the dragonfly and what it was doing. Leave a blank line on the bottom of your entry to add the insect's name later.

DRAGONFLY

Colors: brown thorax, white abdomen

Wing markings: thick black band on

  each wing

Eyes: black

Location/Activity: perched on a flat

  rock near flowers

Insect name: _____

Your Drawing or
Photo Goes Here

❋ Spend about a half hour to an hour on safari (don't forget to drink your water).

❋ Clean up the area and take everything with you when you leave.

At home, download your photos onto the computer and print them. The next chapter will help you identify the dragonflies you found. If you didn't have much luck finding a dragonfly this time, don't get discouraged. Every safari offers new surprises. Try again soon!

THREE
A Guide to Dragonflies

You've had fun on safari and are now ready to identify the dragonflies that crossed your path. The next step is to compare the photos, drawings, and entries in your notebook with the dragonflies on pages 22 and 23. Here's what to do:

Select an entry from your notebook. If you took a photo, now is the time to paste it next to its description. Take a good look at your entry. Ask yourself these questions:

* What is the dragonfly's eye color?
* What color is the thorax? Does it have stripes, spots, or other field markings?
* What color is the abdomen? Are there any field markings? Identifying dragonflies can often be challenging because males and females of the same species may look very different. For instance, a Common Whitetail male has a white body, but the female Common Whitetail has a black and yellow body.
* What shape is the abdomen? Is it pointed at the tip or clublike?

✳ What color are the wings? Even though they may seem clear, look closer. Are the veins tinged red, yellow, or black? How about field markings? Along with the pterostigmata, do the wings have thick bands, black tips, or patches of color?

If you find a match, congratulations! Write its name in your notebook.

DRAGONFLY

Colors: brown thorax, white abdomen

Wing markings: thick black band on

each wing

Eyes: black

Location/Activity: perched on a flat

rock near flowers

Insect name: Common Whitetail (male)

If you can't find your exact dragonfly in the photo guide on pages 22 and 23, don't worry. More than 300 types of dragonflies (and 150 kinds of damselflies) live in North America—far too many to show here.

However, if you can match a few features, like eyes or wings, you still may be able to tell which family your dragonfly belongs to. The major North American dragonfly families are:

* **Skimmers**: Brightly colored with wings that have noticeable field markings. Skimmers tend to be easily found in backyards and parks.
* **Darners**: Large, usually blue or green dragonflies with clear wings. Darners like to hang from trees, bushes, and weeds.
* **Emeralds**: Usually have brown bodies, bright green eyes, and wings with noticeable field markings. Emeralds can blend in around ponds and lakes, making them harder to spot than other dragonflies.
* **Clubtails**: Long, dull brown, yellow, or green bodies, clublike tip on abdomen, and clear wings. Clubtails can be difficult to see as they blend in with rocks and logs on the shoreline.

Dragonfly Guide

SKIMMERS

Blue Dasher

Flame Skimmer

Halloween Pennant

Calico Pennant

Autumn Meadowhawk

DARNERS

Blue-eyed Darner

Shadow Darner

Common Green Darner

Dragonfly Guide

EMERALDS

Prince Baskettail

Mocha Emerald

Common Baskettail

CLUBTAILS

Cobra Clubtail

Eastern Ringtail
Dogface

Russet-tipped Clubtail

FOUR

Try This!
Projects You Can Do

Dragonflies are not only beautiful to watch, but are useful, too. They eat large amounts of gnats, flies, and other insects, helping to keep these populations under control. They are the main predators of mosquitoes, insects that can bite humans and animals and may spread diseases. Scientists also look to dragonflies to reveal clues about our environment. When larvae die off, it can mean the water or soil is unhealthy.

Saving Dragonflies

Scientists say 15 percent, or about forty-five kinds, of North American dragonflies, are in danger of disappearing. The Hine's Emerald is the first dragonfly to be placed on the Federal List of Endangered Species. This means the dragonfly is now protected by the U.S. government, because it is rare and may become **extinct**. At one time, the Hine's Emerald could be spotted in seven states throughout the Midwest. Today, this lovely green-eyed dragonfly can be found only in Illinois, Michigan, Missouri, and Wisconsin.

Even so, humans have put dragonflies at risk. Human development is slowly wiping out the wetlands, ponds, rivers, and streams that dragonflies need to live and breed. Fertilizers, pesticides, and other chemicals seep into water sources, killing larvae and the insects dragonflies feed on. What can you do to make a difference? Help protect the wetlands and waterways in your area. Only use **organic** pesticides and fertilizers in your garden. Also, try some of the projects in this chapter.

Dragonfly Pond

Create a miniature pond for dragonflies to perch, drink, and, perhaps, snack on a tasty insect. Here's what you will need:

* a 7-inch by 9-inch rectangular microwavable food tray or any large, plastic container that's divided into two equal sections
* potting soil
* a few small sticks
* several gravel-sized rocks
* two, small (2-inch) pond-edge plants, such as milkweed, sedge, or rush

In one side of the tray, place the plants in the potting soil. Place the sticks vertically into the soil (for dragonfly perching). In the other side of the tray, line the bottom with the gravel-sized rocks. Fill this side with 1 to 2 inches of water. Select a sunny spot in your garden for your mini pond. Keep the water tray clean and full. Stay on the look-out for water-loving dragonflies!

Flower Garden

A flower garden is not only pretty, but will also attract the insects that dragonflies like to eat. Choose six to eight plants from the list on page 27. Pick a sunny spot in your yard for your garden. Use potting soil from the store. Water your garden every morning. Never use pesticides (you don't want to kill the insects dragonflies eat). Count how many dragonflies come to the garden for a visit and a meal on a summer's day!

A sure way to attract dragonflies to your yard is to start a garden with their favorite plants.

Dragonfly Favorite Plant List

Aster, black-eyed Susan, coneflower, cosmos, daisy, foxglove, heliotrope, lavender, marigold, rose, zinnia, fountain grass (or any type of tall, ornamental grass).

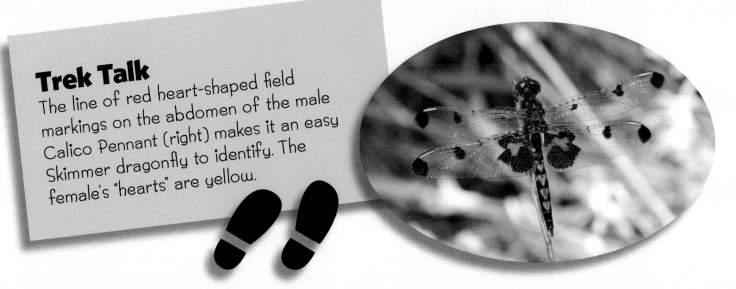

Trek Talk
The line of red heart-shaped field markings on the abdomen of the male Calico Pennant (right) makes it an easy Skimmer dragonfly to identify. The female's "hearts" are yellow.

Perching Stations

Many dragonflies perch on the tops of tall grasses and stems, waiting for their next meal to fly by. A great way to observe dragonflies is to give them a place to perch in your backyard. Find three thin sticks about 4 feet in height. Bamboo sticks work quite well. These can be bought for a few dollars at your local garden center. Choose a sunny spot in your yard that has tall flowers, tall grasses, or medium-sized shrubs.

Build a perching station in your yard. See how many dragonflies it attracts.

Place the sticks in the ground several feet apart. That's it! Check the tops of the sticks often on warm summer days. It's not uncommon for a dragonfly to pick a favorite perch and hang out there all afternoon hunting for food. Remember, if you approach and the dragonfly flies away, stay very still, and the insect will most likely return to its perch in a minute.

Watching dragonflies for fun and participating in dragonfly counts for science are fast becoming popular outdoor activities. Now that you know how to look for dragonflies, chances are you'll start noticing these wispy-winged insects everywhere you go. Why not keep adding your new discoveries to your journal? Imagine how many different dragonflies you'll spot in a month, a year, or even a lifetime!

Glossary

bask	to soak up heat from the sun
exoskeleton	the hard, protective outer covering of an insect
extinct	no longer existing
field markings	spots, bands, stripes, or other distinguishing marks on an animal
larva	a young dragonfly; also called nymph or naiad
mandibles	the jaws of an insect
metamorphosis	the complete change in structure and form of an animal
migrate	to move from one region to another with the changing seasons
molt	the process of growth by which a dragonfly larva sheds its exoskeleton
organic	a substance that is animal or vegetable in origin
prey	animals that are hunted by other animals for food
pterostigmata	small marks or spots on an animal
wingspan	the distance between the two wingtips of a flying animal

Find Out More

Books

Lockwood, Sophie. *Dragonflies.* Mankato, MN: Child's World, 2008.

Nelson, Robin. *Dragonflies.* Minneapolis, MN: Lerner, 2009.

Peters, Elisa. *It's a Dragonfly!* New York: PowerKids Press, 2009.

Websites

BioKIDS: Dragonflies

www.biokids.umich.edu/critters/Anisoptera

Learn more about dragonfly behavior, life cycle, and habitat at the University of Michigan's educational website. Don't miss the stunning gallery of photos of adult dragonflies perching and in flight.

EEK (Environmental Education for Kids): Dragonflies

http://dnr.wi.gov/org/caer/ce/eek/critter/insect/dragonfly.htm

Discover interesting facts and stats about damselflies and dragonflies at this site hosted by the Wisconsin Department of Natural Resources.

Odonata Central

http://odonatacentral.org

www.odonatacentral.org/index.php/GalleryAction.browse

Supported by the Texas Natural Science Center at the University of Texas, Odonata Central offers dragonfly checklists, maps, and an image library. Browse the dragonfly photo gallery to help identify your dragonflies. You can even submit your own photos to add to the collection.

Index

Page numbers in **boldface** are illustrations.

About the Author

TRUDI STRAIN TRUEIT is a former television news reporter and weather anchor, who loves writing about and photographing nature. She has authored more than seventy fiction and nonfiction books for children, including *Birds, Beetles,* and *Slugs, Snails, and Worms* in the Backyard Safari series. She can't wait for the summer months, when Flame Skimmers, Blue-eyed Darners, and other colorful dragonflies visit her yard (she lives near a creek). Trudi grew up in Seattle, Washington, and still lives in the Northwest with her husband, a high school photography teacher. Visit her website at www.truditrueit.com.